Helen Marlais'
# Succeeding at the Piano®
## A Method for Everyone

## For the Student

Throughout this book you will do many different activities such as:

**Writing:**

After you write the answers, you can play them on the piano.

**Rhythm:**

Just as this boy and girl walk in rhythm together, you will feel the steady beat in every rhythm activity!

**Time to Compose:**

Your very own compositions can be just as important as the pieces you learn.

**Ear Training:**

Learn notes and patterns in music by using your ears carefully.

**Follow the Leader**

Use your ears to h...
*rhythmic* patterns.

**Parrot Play:**

Use your ears to hear *musical* patterns.

Production: Frank J. Hackinson
Production Coordinators: Joyce Loke and Satish Bhakta
Editors: Joyce Loke, Edwin McLean, and Peggy Gallagher
Art Direction: Andi Whitmer – in collaboration with Helen Marlais
Cover Illustration: ©2012 Susan Hellard/Arena
Interior Illustrations: ©2010 Susan Hellard/Arena
                        ©2012 Teresa Robertson/Arena
Cover and Interior Illustration Concepts: Helen Marlais
Engraving: Tempo Music Press, Inc.
Printer: Tempo Music Press, Inc.

ISBN-13: 978-1-56939-995-8

# Grade 3 - Table of Contents

# The Mysterious Bookcase

**(Review of Music Symbols and Terms from Grade 2B)**

- In an attic, a mysterious bookcase is locked.
- You find the key for the lock in a floorboard!
- Once you open it, you see music symbols and terms that have been hidden for hundreds of years!
- Draw a line from the musical symbol or term on the right and left shelves to the correct answer on the middle shelf.

# Pirate's Gold
## (Review of Intervals and Note Names)

- Draw an X on the nearest guide note.
- Name the intervals and notes.
- Then draw a line from each gold coin to the correct interval.

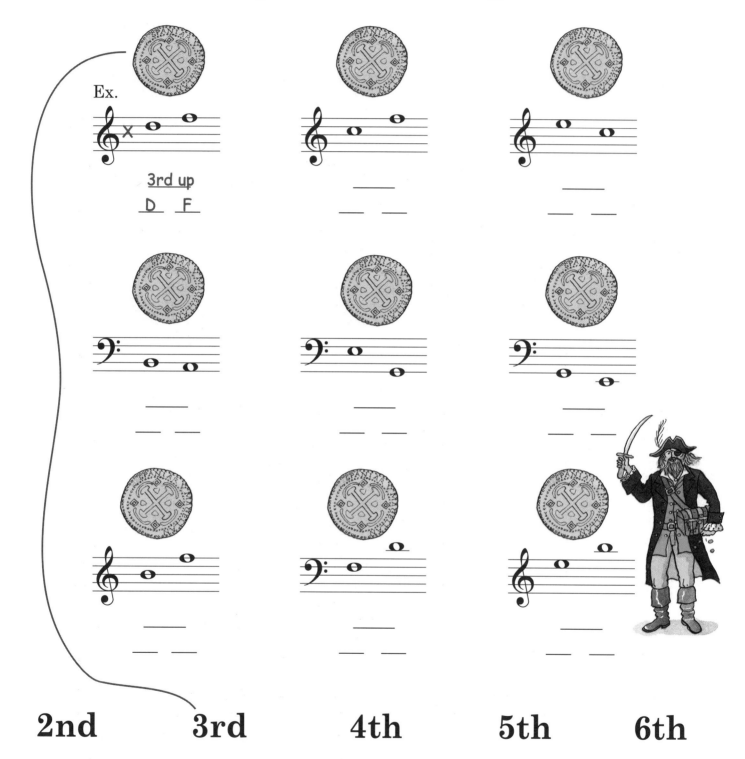

Ex.

3rd up
D  F

**2nd**    **3rd**    **4th**    **5th**    **6th**

**Extra Credit:**

- These 2 patterns are made up of:
  2nds    3rds    4ths (circle one)

# Review of the I-V⁷-I Cadence in Major Keys

- Draw a line from each cadence (I-V⁷-I) to its correct key.
- Then circle the leading tone in every V⁷ chord.
  (Remember the leading one is always a half step below the tonic.)

Key of:

F Major

D Major

C Major

A Major

G Major

Now play **all** of the cadences!

# ⅜ Time Signature

Mu-sic is won - der - ful!

In ⅜ time, there are 3 beats in each measure.   The ♪ = 1 beat

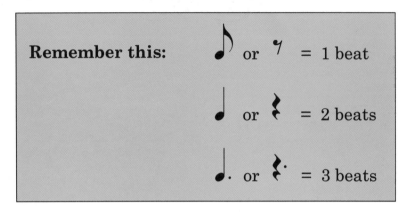

**Remember this:**   ♪ or 𝄾 = 1 beat

♩ or 𝄼 = 2 beats

♩. or 𝄼· = 3 beats

**1.** Finish the counting in each rhythm pattern below. Then clap and count aloud, whispering the rests.

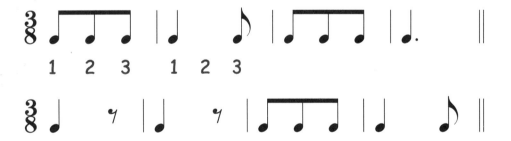

1  2  3   1  2  3

**2.** Add bar lines to each pattern below. Then tap and count aloud, with the metronome.

Andante (♪ = 112)   Moderato (♪ = 138)   Allegro (♪ = 168)

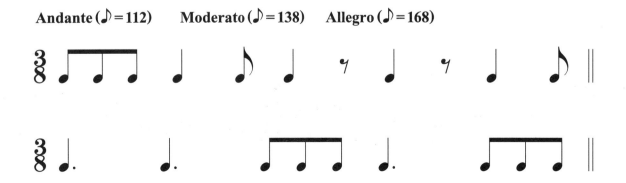

FJH2073

## Parrot Play:

Parrots love to repeat what they hear!

- Your teacher will play a pattern from each set below.
- Which pattern do you hear, a or b?
- Play the one you hear.
- Then circle it.

## Ear Training:

- Your teacher will play either a or b.
- Which pattern do you hear?
- Play the one you hear.
- Circle it.

## Time to Compose:

- Make up your own piece using $\frac{3}{8}$ time.
- Include repeated notes in the melody.
- Use I and V⁷ chords in the harmony.
- Will it be AB or ABA form?
  (Binary)    (Ternary)

My title: _____

**UNIT 2**

# $\frac{6}{8}$ Time Signature

**6** — 6 beats in every measure
**8** — ♪ (𝄾) = 1 beat

**1.** Clap and count aloud with energy!

**2.** Add the bar lines and finish the counting.
Point to each note and count aloud.

**3.** Write in the counting below.
Circle the measures that have too many beats.
Fix the measures by drawing in the correct beats and then clap and count aloud.

FJH2073

# Two Famous Themes

Checklist for Mozart and Beethoven.
Place a ✔ once you have finished each point below.

_____ 1. Write the counting in each theme.

_____ 2. Write the letter name above each note.

_____ 3. Silently play each theme on the top of the keys.

_____ 4. Play each theme while **counting aloud**.

_____ 5. Transpose each theme to another key.

## Horn Concerto
by Wolfgang Amadeus Mozart

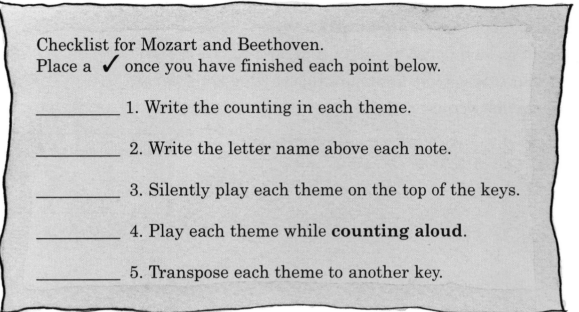

## Symphony No. 6
### "Shepherd's Song"
by Ludwig van Beethoven

**Follow the Leader:**

$\frac{6}{8}$ time is considered to be a **compound meter**.

- It can be felt as having two beats per measure. ($\downarrow$. = 1 beat).
- Listen to your teacher clap and count this rhythm both ways.
- Then repeat what you hear.

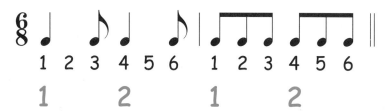

Feel the natural accents on beats 1 and 4 and you'll have it.

# Over the River and Through the Woods

Traditional

Lyrics by Lydia Maria Child

- Clap and count the rhythm, saying "**1** 2 3 **4** 5 6," slightly accenting beats 1 and 4.
- Then, say the words while clapping 2 beats per measure.
- Lastly, clap the rhythm of the song while saying aloud, "1 – 2."

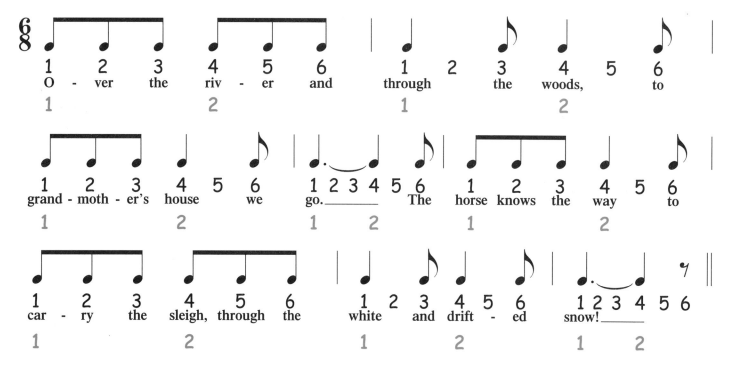

**Helpful Hint:**

It may be helpful to set up a metronome click when doing these exercises.

**Follow the Leader:**

- Listen to your teacher clap the rhythms on the right. Watch the music!

- Can you clap them back?

**Parrot Play:**

- Your teacher will clap the following rhythms. (S)he will add a pattern from the box to the empty measures.

- Clap the pattern you hear in the empty measures, and then write it in.

- Lastly, clap and count aloud the entire line.

For teacher use:

# The Primary Triads

- The IV chord (called "4" chord) is built on the 4th note of the scale.

- You already know that the V chord (called "5" chord) is built on the 5th of the scale.

- These 3 triads are in ROOT POSITION.

- Play them.

- Write the correct Roman numeral below each triad.

Key of C Major:

_____   _____   _____   _____

_____   _____   _____   _____

- Draw the following triads in C Major.

I triad:      IV triad:

---

**Quick Quiz:**

**1.** In G Major:

What is the I triad? _____G_____

What is the IV triad? _____

What is the V triad? _____

**2.** In F Major:

What is the I triad? _____

What is the IV triad? _____

What is the V triad? _____

- Now play these triads.

FJH2073

This is the I-IV-I (plagal) cadence:

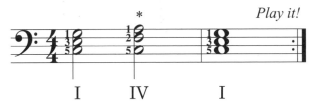

I    IV    I

*Play it!*

- Play these. ———————▶
- Notice that the circled chord is in the I-IV-I cadence above!

The IV chord is changed to an inversion to make it easier to play:

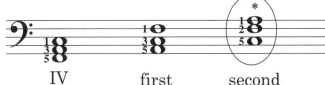

IV
root position

first
inversion

second
inversion

**Ear Training:**

- Play the melody of this folk song.
- Then, by ear, play the I, IV, and V⁷ chords in the L.H.
- Write in the four missing chords and play the entire piece.

# Baa, Baa, Black Sheep

Traditional

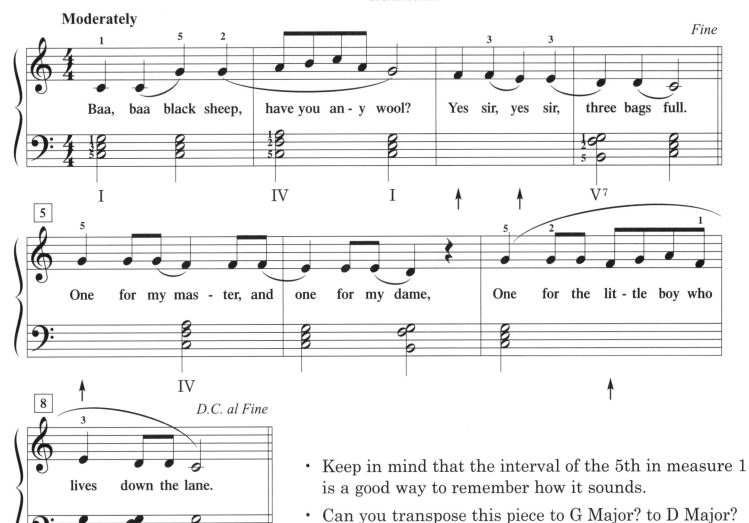

- Keep in mind that the interval of the 5th in measure 1 is a good way to remember how it sounds.
- Can you transpose this piece to G Major? to D Major?

**13**

# The I-IV-I-V⁷-I Cadence in C Major

- Play these cadences while saying the names of the chords.

     I     IV     I   V⁷    I

Say: "one" "four" "one" "five-seven" "one"

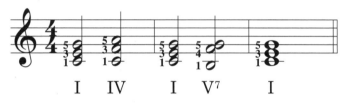

     I     IV     I   V⁷    I

Say: "one" "four" "one" "five-seven" "one"

# Sam has suddenly forgotten the C Major cadence!

- He started to write in the notes of the chords, but has slowed down.
- Help him by writing in the correct notes as well as the fingering.
- Then play the chords while saying the correct fingering aloud.

Ex.

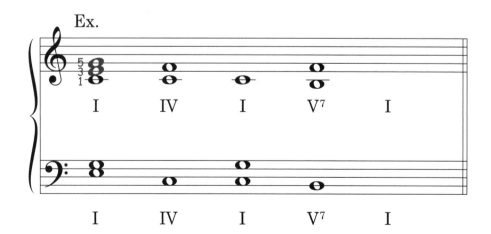

     I     IV     I   V⁷    I

     I     IV     I   V⁷    I

FJH2073

# As Fast as Lightning

- Use a clock and time yourself.
- Play each of these chords of the C Major cadence and write the Roman numeral (I-IV-V⁷) for each chord below.
- The chords are in no particular order – your task is to find them quickly!

Ex.

$\underline{\quad I \quad}$

_____

_____   _____   _____   _____

_____   _____   _____   _____

_____   _____   _____   _____

Your time to complete the entire page: _____ minutes _____ seconds

FJH2073

- There are L.H. chords missing in the piece below.
- Write in the missing chords while you play the piece.

# Five Little Chickadees

Traditional

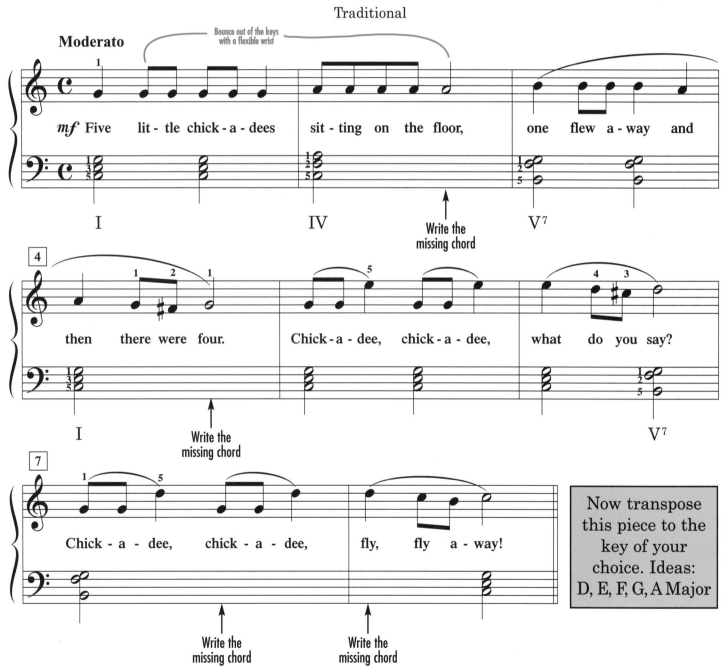

FJH2073

# Ledger Line Notes Review

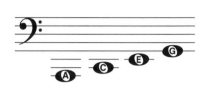

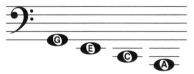

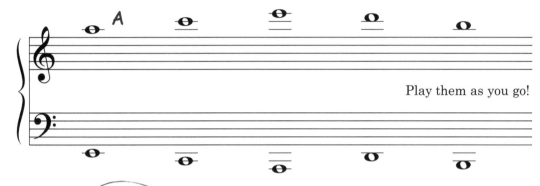

FACE

*George Eats Crunchy Apples*

*All   Cows   Eat   Grass*

• Name the following notes. One has been done for you.

**A**

Play them as you go!

**Time to Compose:**

• Make up your own piece in $\frac{6}{8}$ time. (It has been started for you.)

• Use AA¹ form.

• Use at least one ledger line note in your piece.

• Add a tempo marking and dynamics as well.

## Swaying in a Hammock

# The I-IV-I-V⁷-I Cadence in G Major

- Play these cadences while saying the names of the chords:

I    IV    I    V⁷    I

I    IV    I    V⁷    I

- Now play the cadences with your eyes **closed**.

# The "Empire" of G Major

- Play each chord below. Then write the name of each chord.
- Lastly, draw a line from each chord below to the correct Roman numeral in a coliseum.

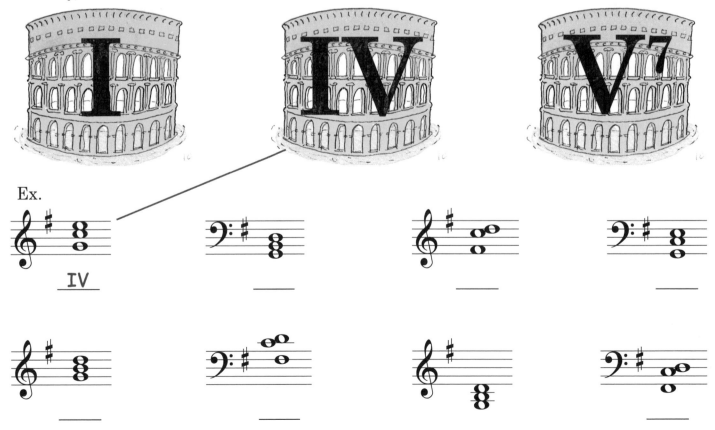

# Intervals

**Keep in mind:** An interval is the distance between two notes.

"Look and think fast"
7ths are made up of 2 notes on 2 lines or 2 spaces.
Octaves are made up of 1 line note and 1 space note.

- Label the intervals below. Then play them.

3rd

- Label these 7ths and octaves in C Major. Then play them.

- Label these 7ths and octaves in G Major. Then play them.

**Ear Training:**

- Your teacher will play some 7ths and octaves.
- Write what you hear, without looking at the piano!

  1. _____   2. _____   3. _____   4. _____

For teacher use: (To be played in any order.)

# More Intervals

- Intervals have different **qualities**.

  Play the following:

C Major:

When a 5th contains **7 half steps**, it is called a Perfect 5th.

- One of the following is **not** a Perfect 5th. Place an X through it.
  Play them to help you decide.

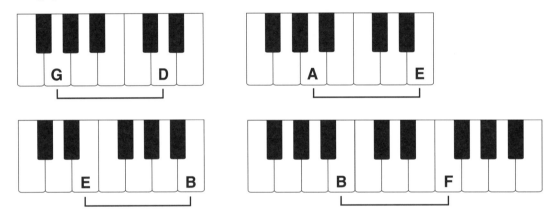

 In the 5th that is **not** a Perfect 5th, raise the upper note by a half step. It is now a Perfect 5th!

 Now play all of these Perfect 5ths!

# Are you READY FOR A CHALLENGE?

- Circle the correct interval below every pattern. Then play them.
- Keep in mind the key you are in.

| 2nd | Major 3rd | minor 3rd | 6th | Octave |
| 3rd | Perfect 4th | Perfect 5th | 7th | 7th |

FJH2068

# Cut Time $\frac{2}{2}$ ¢

- Pieces in cut time are played quickly and with energy.

**Before Playing:**

- Write in the counting for *Russian Dance*.
- Tap hands together, feeling the natural accent on the strong beats.

## Russian Dance
### (Trepak)

from *The Nutcracker*

Pyotr Ilyich Tchaikovsky
1840-1893 Russia

*alla breve* *

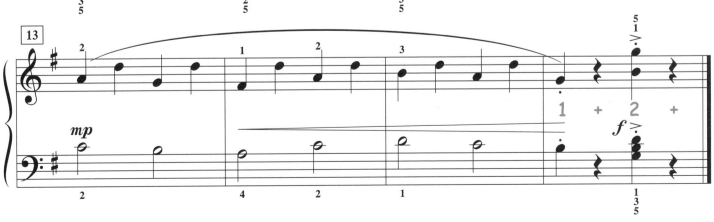

- The form of this piece is: A B A B¹   A B A

(circle one)

* *alla breve* is the same as cut time ($\frac{2}{2}$).

**UNIT 6**

# The I-IV-I-V⁷-I Cadence in F Major

**1.** Only one of the 3 palaces below shows the correct F Major cadence.
Circle the correct palace and cadence. Then play the cadence.

**2.** Write the F Major cadence in the treble staff below. A few notes are added to help you.
Then add the fingering and play it.

**With majesty**

*mf*    I    IV    I    V⁷    I

• The palace above is a picture of the Gyeongbok palace in South Korea.

FJH2073

## Ear Training:

- Your teacher will play two intervals in a row.
  One will be a 7th and the other will be an octave.

- Without looking at the piano, name the first interval, then the second interval.

1. _____ _____    2. _____ _____

For teacher use: (To be played in any order.)

| octave | 7th | | 7th | octave |

## Follow the Leader:

- Listen to your teacher clap a rhythm.
  Do you hear a or b?

- Can you clap it back?

a.

### Parrot Play:

- Your teacher will play any of the following intervals.

- Watch and listen carefully and repeat each one.

  (Note for Teacher: play 2nds, M3rds, m3rds, P4ths, P5ths, 6ths, 7ths, and octaves.)

b.

## Time to Compose:

- Make up a piece in F Major that is cheerful like *Little Mohee*.
- Use I, IV, and V$^7$ chords in a waltz bass pattern.
- Put the melody in your R.H.
- What will your title be? _____

# Triplet

**Triplet** is the word given to
a group of 3 notes that equal a ♩

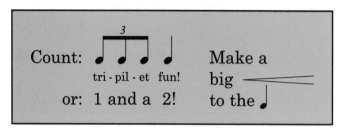

**1.** Add the time signatures below. Then finish adding the counting.
Clap and say the rhythm aloud.
Feel the forward direction to each ♩ that follows a triplet.

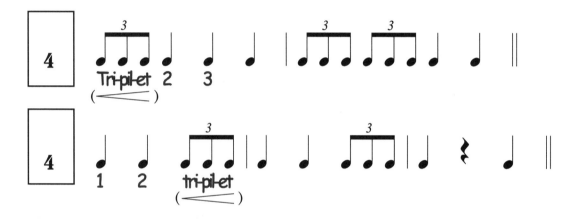

**2.** Some of the measures below are missing notes! Fill them in and then clap and
count with energy.

**Time to Compose:**

- Make up a short piece using triplets.
- Use the key of G Major.
- Decide if it will be fast or slow.

  Your title: _____

FJH2073

# Triplet

- A great way to feel triplet rhythms is
to make a *crescendo* ◁
to the long note that immediately follows the

tri - pil - et fun!

*mf* ◁ *f*

**1.** Clap and speak these phrases.

Here we go now!  Come join a - long!

I like to play  pia - no all day!

**2.** Now play the folk song below. Make a ◁ to each ♩ or 𝅗𝅥 that follows the pattern.

## Sing Together Merrily

Traditional

*Changing fingers on the same key will keep your wrist flexible.*

**Happily**

*mf*

Sing to - geth - er, mer - ri - ly, mer - ri - ly sing,

mer - ri - ly, mer - ri - ly sing, mer - ri - ly, mer - ri - ly,

mer - ri - ly, mer - ri - ly sing!

# How To Keep a Piano Happy

- Fill in the name of the notes to learn the facts.

TO   K _ _ P   _   PI _ NO   _ T   ITS   _ _ ST,

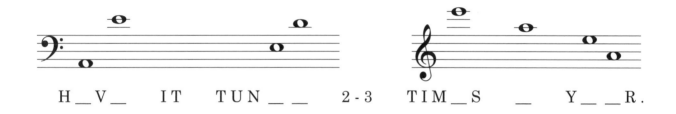

H _ V _   IT   TUN _ _   2 - 3   TIM _ S   _   Y _ _ R.

K _ _ P   IT   _ L _ _ N   (INSIDE AND OUT!),   K _ _ P

IT   _ T   _   ST _ _ _ _ Y   T _ MP _ R _ TUR _,

_ N _   PL _ Y   IT   R _ _ UL _ RLY!

**Extra Credit:** Play all of the notes on the piano!

FJH2073

# Review of Accompaniment Patterns in the L.H.

**Waltz Bass**     **Broken Triad Bass**     **Alberti Bass**

bottom top middle top

**How Much Do You Know?** (Earn 1 point for each correct answer.)

1. Write the key below.
2. Label the harmony (I, IV, or V⁷.)

3. Play each one!
4. Write the kind of bass (waltz, broken triad, Alberti.)

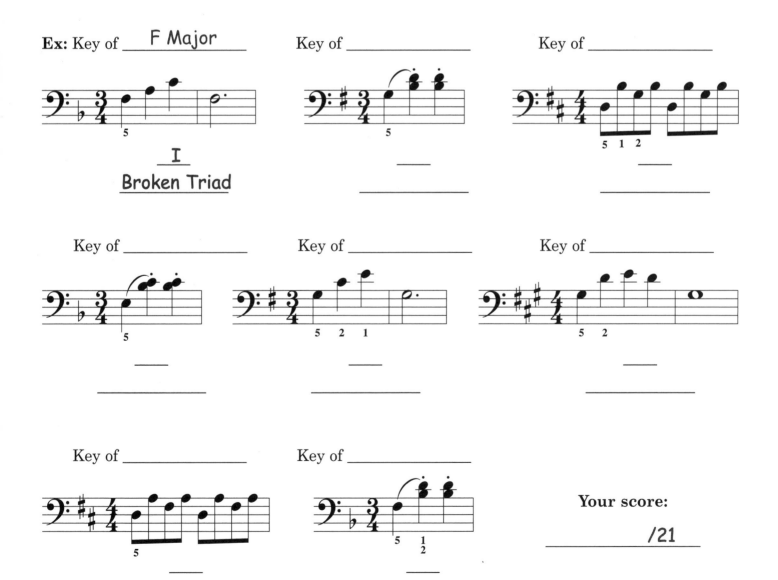

**Ex:** Key of ____F Major____

I

Broken Triad

Key of _____

Key of _____

Key of _____

Key of _____

Key of _____

Key of _____

Key of _____

**Your score:**

_____ /21

# The Chromatic Scale

- The chromatic octave scale is made up entirely of half steps.
- It uses every key in the octave—black and white.
- A chromatic scale can start on any key.

# FINGERING FRENZY!

**1.** Two fingerings are incorrect in each chromatic octave scale below.
Correct them and then play the scale *legato* while saying the correct fingering aloud.

**Keep in mind:** For every **black key**, use finger 3.
For every **two white keys** in a row:  R.H. going up, use fingers 1-2.
L.H. going down, use fingers 1-2.

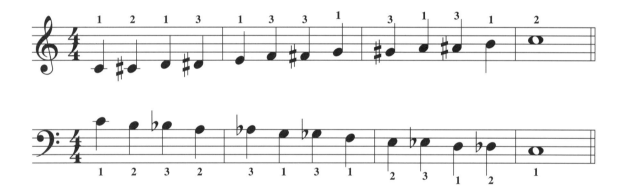

When passages
go up, use ♯'s.
When passages go down,
use ♭'s.

**2.** One note in every chromatic passage is incorrect. (The fingering is correct.)
Fix the note and then play the pattern.

# At the Band Concert

- You and a friend will go to a band concert soon!
- Draw a line from each note on the left to its **enharmonic** match on the right.

# Review of Ledger Line Notes Above the Treble Staff

# The Trapeze Artist

- Help the trapeze artist jump to the trapeze on the other side.
- Name the following intervals and notes. A perfect score means she will not fall in the net.

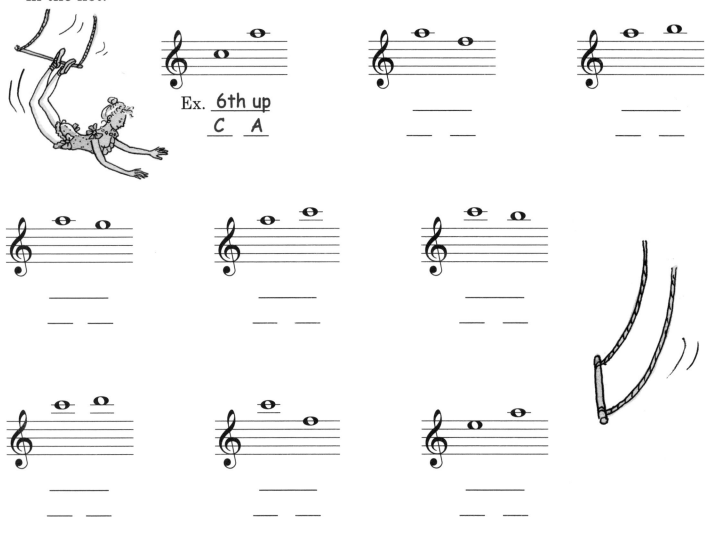

Ex. 6th up
C   A

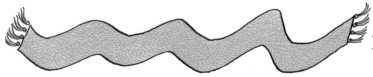

Now play **all** the patterns on this page!

FJH2073

# Review of Ledger Line Notes Below the Bass Staff

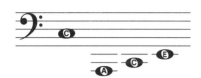

# The Professional Diver

- The diver wants to find a rare fish at the bottom of the sea.

- Name the following intervals and notes. A perfect score means he will find the rare fish.

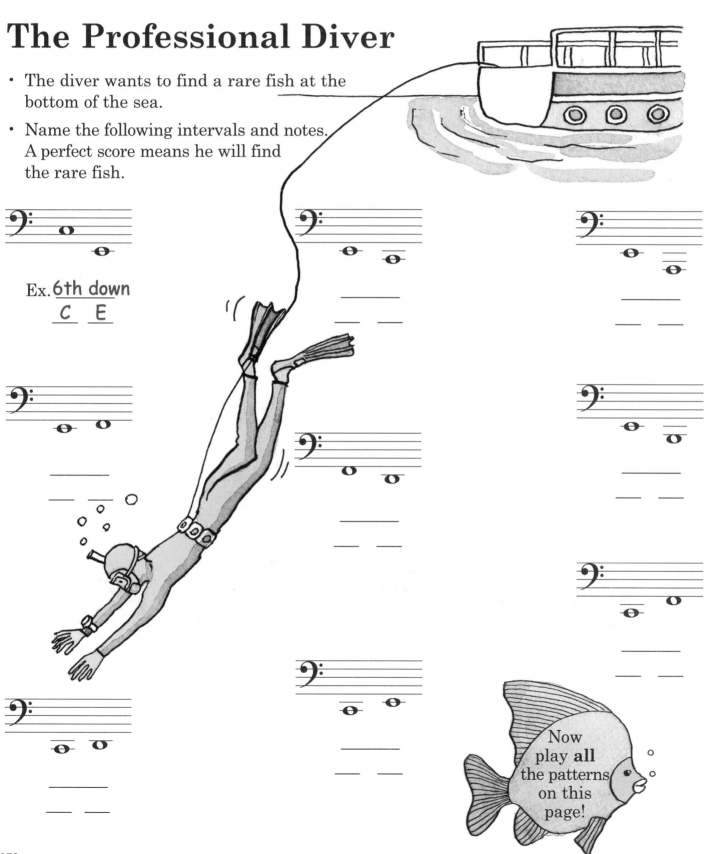

Ex. 6th down
C   E

Now play **all** the patterns on this page!

# The Key of A Minor

- A minor is the relative key of C Major. Both keys have no ♯'s or ♭'s.
- There are 3 forms of minor – NATURAL, HARMONIC, and MELODIC.

## Natural Minor

- Write the A minor scale in the L.H. to match the R.H. Add the fingering.
  Then play hands together.

## Harmonic Minor — the 7th note is raised by one half step.

- With a **colored** pencil, add accidentals to the natural minor scale above to make it the harmonic form. Then play it hands together.

## Melodic Minor — the 6th and 7th notes are raised one half step on the way up, and lowered on the way down.

- Play the melodic minor scale below.
- Draw a line from each balloon to the correct notes in the melodic minor scale.
  (5 balloons will have **two** strings attached to notes.)

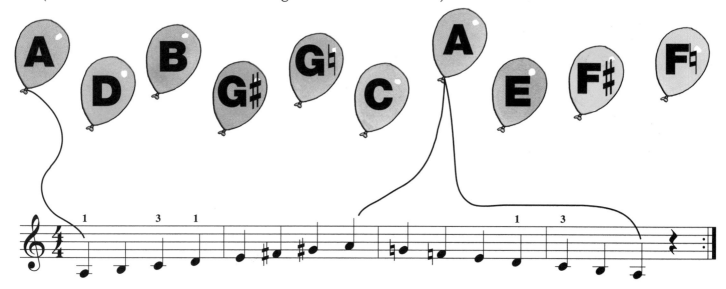

FJH2073

# In the Amazon Jungle

• As you meet the living creatures in the jungle, complete the music examples.

**1.** **As you pass a jaguar:**

- Complete the A minor cadence in the L.H.
- Add the fingering. Then play it.

**2.** **As you gaze at macaws:**

- Complete the A minor cadence in the R.H.
- Add the fingering. Then play it.

**3.** **As you laugh with the spider monkeys:**

- Play the following minor scale.
- Circle the correct form.

natural    harmonic    melodic

**4.** **And as you run from the anaconda:**

- Play the following minor scale.
- Circle the correct form.

natural    harmonic    melodic

**Ear Training:**

**1.**

- Your teacher will play major and minor scales.
- Without looking at the piano, write what you hear: M for major, m for minor.

  1. _____    2. _____

  3. _____    4. _____

**2.**

- Now your teacher will play minor scales.
- Without looking at the piano, write what form you hear: natural, harmonic, or melodic.

  1. _____    2. _____

  3. _____    4. _____

# In Search of Sequences

- When a phrase is immediately repeated one step lower or higher, it is called a **sequence**.

- Play the examples below, and write in the notes that will make the next sequence correct.

**1.**

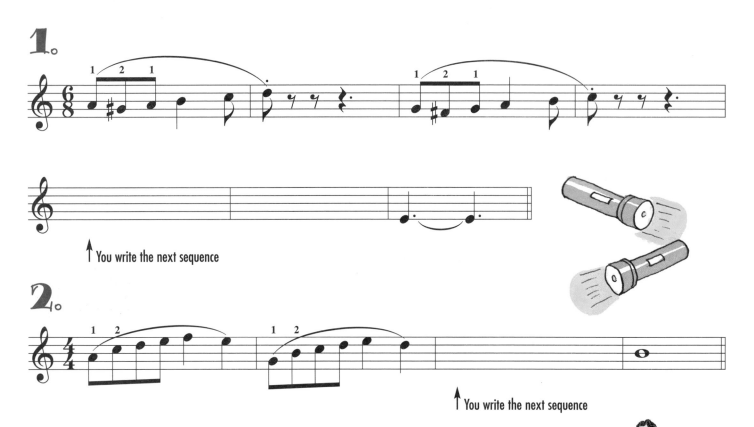

↑ You write the next sequence

**2.**

↑ You write the next sequence

# A Famous Melody in A Minor

**Before Playing:**

- Mark the form in the music. Is it AA[1], AB, or ABA?

- Circle the only melodic 6th.

## Waltz
(KK IVb, No. 11)

Frédéric Chopin
1810-1849, Poland

FJH2073

# Review of Triads and Inversions

- To make a triad (or chord) easier to play in a cadence, the notes are moved to different positions. They are **inverted**.

- Look at the sun, star, and moon below. Notice how the symbol at the bottom moves to the top in every inversion.

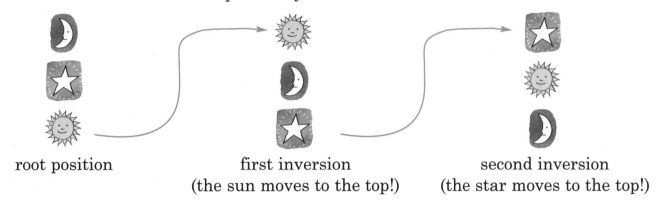

root position

first inversion
(the sun moves to the top!)

second inversion
(the star moves to the top!)

Now look at a D minor triad:
(IV in A minor)

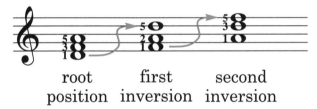

root
position

first
inversion

second
inversion

Review the "sunshine exercise" from p. 9 of your *Lesson Book* so that this is easy!

- Write the D minor triad and its inversions for the left hand.
- Add the fingering.

root
position

first
inversion

second
inversion

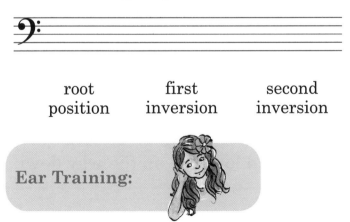

**Ear Training:**

- Your teacher will play major and minor triads.
- Without looking at the piano, write "M" for major and "m" for minor.

1. _____    2. _____    3. _____

**Extra Credit:** If your teacher plays a triad and its inversions, can you tell if it's in root, first, or second inversion?

# The Key of D Minor

- D minor is the relative key of F Major.
  Walk three half steps up from D and you find F.
- Both keys have one flat – B♭.

## Natural Minor

- Write the D minor scale in the R.H. to match
  the L.H. Add the fingering.
  Then play hands together.

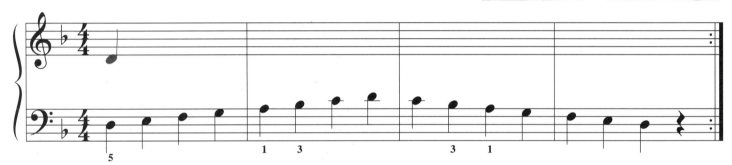

## Harmonic Minor — the 7th note is raised by _____ step.

- With a **colored** pencil, add accidentals to the natural minor scale above to make it
  harmonic. Then play it hands together.

## Melodic Minor — the _____ and _____ notes are raised one half
step on the way up, and lowered on the way down.

- Four notes are missing in the melodic scale below.
- Write them in and then play the scale.

# The D Minor Cadence

Play the cadence with your R.H.

i  iv  i  V⁷  i

- Complete the D minor cadence in the L.H. Circle the leading tone.
- Add the fingering and then play.

i  iv  i  V⁷  i

# Listening Experience

- Play the three forms of D minor scales for three different people.

  Ask them how each form is **different** to them. Ask them to think about their **color, mood,** and **shape**.

| <u>NATURAL FORM</u> | <u>HARMONIC FORM</u> | <u>MELODIC FORM</u> |
|---|---|---|
| _____ | _____ | _____ |
| _____ | _____ | _____ |
| _____ | _____ | _____ |

**Time to Compose:**

- It's time for you to compose your own *Tarantella*.
- Think of the mood of the piece. A few ideas are written below. Will you use the natural, harmonic, or melodic minor form?
- Once you have learned it, record it!

MOODS  light  bright  happy!

energetic!  CHEERFUL!  ANGRY!

quiet

sad  joyful!  thoughtful

My title: _____

# Hall of Fame—
# Know the Composers

- You know many famous composers now!
- Say all of their names for your teacher and notice when they lived.
- The composers that are ★'d are new for this grade.
- Choose one **new** composer and tell your teacher something about him.

## Baroque Era
### (c. 1600 - c. 1750)

## Classical Era
### (c. 1750 - c. 1820)

**Antonio Vivaldi**

**Franz Joseph Haydn**

**Wolfgang Amadeus Mozart**

**Ludwig van Beethoven**

## Romantic Era
### (c. 1820 - c. 1900)

**Niccolò Paganini**
(Lesson Book, p. 50)

**Frédéric Chopin**

**Robert Schumann**

**38**

FJH2073

# Romantic Era (continued)
## (c. 1820 - c. 1900)

**Johann Strauss, Jr.**
(Lesson Book, p. 4)

**Alexander
Borodin**

**Johannes Brahms**

**Camille Saint-Saëns**

**Georges Bizet**

**Antonín Dvořák**
(Lesson Book, p. 20)

# 20th/21st Centuries
## (c. 1900 - present)

**John Philip Sousa**
(Lesson Book, p. 46)

**Ignace Paderewski**
(Lesson Book, p. 37)

**Scott Joplin**
(Recital Book, p. 26)

**Aaron Copland**

# Certificate of Achievement

_____

Student

has completed

Helen Marlais'
## Succeeding at the Piano®

## Theory and Activity Book
# GRADE 3

You are now ready for
# GRADE 4

_____          _____

Date                                    Teacher's Signature

THE
F·J·H
MUSIC
COMPANY
INC.

Frank J. Hackinson